The Last Green Valley

The Last Green Valley

Poems by Barbara Thomas

Cherry Grove

Barbara Thomas
October 2, 2021

Published by Cherry Grove Collections
P.O. Box 541106
Cincinnati, OH 45254-1106

ISBN: 978-1-62549-327-9

Poetry Editor: Kevin Walzer
Business Editor: Lori Jareo

Visit us on the web at www.cherry-grove.com

Acknowledgements

The author would like to thank the following journals and presses for publishing a number of poems in this book.

The Paterson Literary Review 2014-2015: "Wild Music"

Fiele-Festa 2015: "Melina's Taverna"

Seduced by Sighs of Trees

Cloudkeeper Press, 2007: "Konitza," "Santorini Blue," "Haying"

My deepest gratitude to my writers' group for their friendship, encouragement, and support in my writing and revision and faith in me. Elizabeth Quinlan, Deborah Pheiffer, and Ruby Polterak. I want to thank other past members, Molly-Lynn Watt, Dorothy Nelson, Bernadette Davidson, Holly Guran.

I want to thank members and teachers of the William Joiner Center Writers' Workshop at U/Mass, Boston for their support, encouragement and fellowship. Martha Collins for her friendship, meticulous editing and seeing the arc of this book, Fred Marchant for his kind suggestions, great teaching and inspiration.

I would like to thank my dear friends and family for their unwavering support; my brother David Thomas, "Aunt Penna", Helen Thomas.

Dedicated to my family

Table of Contents

...to live on the fragrance of the earth
and like the air plant be sweetened by light.

Sherwood Anderson (1876-1941)

Northern Epirus

a place of boundary disputes
a borderland
a place that is no longer
the place my mother was born

The geography of my mother's homeland
imprints my mind with washes of color;
verdant green, stone gray for mountains,
emerald for the Aoös River.

Air so fresh you can taste it my mother said.
She lived with her mother, father, uncles, grandmother
in a great stone farmhouse.
They raised sheep for wool, wheat for grain.
When she drew water from the community well,
she saw veiled women carrying urns on their heads,
tinkers who came by.

They celebrated baptisms, namedays, weddings.
Her face was radiant when she spoke of violets

by rushing streams, picnics, her beloved grandmother.

When my mother was twelve
Greek schools closed,
brother betrayed brother,
Her father, in New York City for five years
to earn money came back
and in a ship of thousands brought his family to America.

At my grandmother's each Sunday
we are full of avgolemeno soup, chicken, baklava.
We crack red eggs on Easter,
look for the Good Luck Quarter
in the meat pie on New Years Day.
 We don't talk about times in Northern Epirus,
now southern Albania.

Voices

reach my bedroom window
relatives and neighbors
gather by the weeping willow
summer evenings

for coffee and stories

how my pregnant grandmother
lost her baby on the big ship
her wails unheard

how my grandfather
farmer cab driver store owner
brought his two brothers over

how he bought land
twenty acres of
hills valleys fields

cows goats chickens pigs
two pintos

how the town took much of it away
for a penny for flood control

how the children played
blessed the land

America

my Aunt Annette's gutteral laugh
floats up with
the night song of crickets

Kourambeithes

We mix flour, egg, clove, dash of brandy
smooth and shape flaky dough
into stars, hearts and diamonds,
rolling twists and turns.

As the kourambiethes bake
you tell me stories of your life
in a mountain village in Northern Epirus
 by the green river Aoös
walks with your donkey
week long wedding celebrations
with feasting and dancing.

While the kourambiedes bake,
toasty comfort floats from the stove.
Later, we put them on racks to cool,
dust them with powdered sugar.

Your mother taught you
the lesson of kourambiedes

by the hearth in the stone farmhouse
near fields of wheat, the singing of wild birds.

She took you across the ocean
to a gray shingled house
in a busy mill town
where you baked in her immaculate kitchen.

Texture by touch
shape by sight
the recipe passes on.

Nameday

Father Luke blesses the icon of St. George
swinging the gold censer. Scented smoke

lingers in the air. He presses a white carnation
in my father's hand to honor him and his namesake.

Later at our home when relatives come to celebrate,
I serve the tray of hospitality:

korambeides, baklava, cherry spoon sweets,
grapes, baklava, slices of melon.

I balance tall water glasses and kadahs of whiskey
that the men drink down in a single gulp.

I swerve around the room
greeting each guest.

A scoop of spoon sweet, a click of silver
in an emptied glass, I move to the next guest.

Old Doxie, a widow in black homespun, wild hair,
pinches both my cheeks. It hurts, but I don't flinch.
Despina whispers, "she's so poised."
A look of pride on my mother's face.

Uncle Jimmy laughs, gives a toast of good will:
"Varvara, I will dance at your wedding."

In My Grandfather's House

he sits in his worn chair watching window weather
the room is dark and quiet
the only sound the click of his worry beads

day's chores are done
chickens fed horses in their stalls
goats in their hay filled pens

my grandmother churns butter
cream colored and smooth

the smell of baking bread

Baklava

My grandmother begins at dawn
rolling layers of thin filo;
she brushes each one
with warm yellow butter,
the crush of nuts and honey.

Its ambrosial nectar caresses my tongue.
Music of northern mountains
Mediterranean sun
forgiveness from the sea
in each bite.

I see a faint smile
on her stern smooth face,
waist-length hair
plaited and pinned in a bun.

Outside in the small yard
the stream runs free.

Mother's Day

Wild violets cluster
beneath the juniper bushes
in the front yard

 along the stonewall
in the back yard
where Cleo is buried

I follow a trail of violets
to the riverbank
near the bridge

stop by the brook
gurgling on both sides of the road
where almost hidden

in the tall green grasses
I smell the fragrance
of amber and breath of rose

I walk as far as the cleft in the hill

near Aunt Olgas

where the white lilacs grow

make a bouquet of purple and white flowers

for you

Air

My mother often raved about the air
in the mountains of Northern Epirus.
So fresh you can taste it.

Do you ever feel ecstatic about air?

I do on Fabyan Road
in the Quiet Corner
in the Last Green Valley,

especially after rainstorms,
early morning walks by the Quinebaug
to see the great blue heron.

I did once in Yellowstone
driving along Yellowstone Lake
driving along the Madison River

new vistas at every turn

immense valleys and grassland

shades of green undulating in sunlight.

My mother often raved about the air.

My Mother's Table

I see her in the kitchen,
spoon in hand, tasting, adding spice.
Her cooking sustains us still.

Avgolemeno Soup
Spanikopeta
Korambeides
Baklava
Trahana

Chicken and Rice Pilaf
Baked Lamb
Salata
Dolma
Shish Kebab

Spaghetti and Meatballs
Hot Turkey Sandwich
Potato Salad
Hamburgers

Hot Dogs

Greek Style, Albanian Style, American Style

Fabyan Village

Beyond our backyard hedge
my grandfather's garden of abundance,
in one corner red, orange, yellow gladioli
that often grace our table.

Beyond the garden are wire pens
for chickens, pigs and goats.

Beyond the pens a creaking wooden gate
opens to the hills
where two pintos, Penny and Spotty, graze.

Twenty acres
where we play in hills valleys and fields
from the canal that flows to the Quinebaug
to Oakerson's stone wall boundary.

We name our special places:

    Lookout Point where I
    run up the hill for the birdnest view

queen of all I survey.

Blue Valley, a dip and sweep of land where
I wander to sing and the horses roam.

Sandstone Hill, a cutaway sandbank where we jump
into spilling sands, choose stones for hopscotch.

Before it changed.

Before the town took the land for flood control.
Before the vines wrapped around trees
and wilted goldenrods tangled into wild brush
hiding coyotes and foxes.

Living alone in grandfather's white house
my aunt Penna still serves welcoming cups of coffee.
At the door a new blonde collie barks at strangers.

The Sheltering

Next door grandfather sits
on his worn chair by the window.

I hear strains of Epiroti music
as I walk by on the stone path:
the clarinet's lament
the bouzouki's wail.

Aunt Penna is driving her tractor
the hay-baler rhythmically dropping
honey colored squares onto the field.

My grandmother is baking:
that fragrance wafts thru the open door.
I am tempted to stay for bread
and homemade butter,

but the pasture where the horses graze
call me, the valley where I go to sing
among wild goldenrod and daisies,
underbrush burrs sticking to my clothes and skin.

Along the canal vines hang like snakes.
We swing on them up and over this meandering
waterway that leads to the Quinebaug.

If there is wholeness it is here,
the smell of cut hay   wind thru trees
the river
the sun on my back.

Eyes Everywhere

after Pastures of Memory by Davlov Ipcar

Young girl with long yellow hair
in the middle of a pasture
her eyes watching
svelte horses
a brown cow
a black cat hunting
a golden dog running
a meadowlark in flight
yellow-brown butterflies
gossamer wings of the dragonfly
leaves teal gold burgundy blue
smell of sumac and earth.

Summer edges into fall.

Wild hearts beat with hers
animals birds insects flowers,
life cycles contained
connect with each other.

The gray horse prances,

the red stallion waits.

Nature spends herself renewing.

The girl is in the middle of abundance

eyes wide open.

The Falls

Fabyan Village, 1950

You cross the bridge onto a path through the woods,
where a stream leads to a waterfall
where you clear dead leaves from the rock ledge
as water cascades to the basin below
and you go down a steep incline to a place
of coolness, damp and redolent with evergreens
and step gingerly into knee deep water
until you are standing on a flat slab
under the sheet of icy water
fragrant with pine
drenching your hair, back, legs
penetrating your sweat-soaked skin
and you notice the wild ferns and mossy boulders,
you think you are in a primeval paradise
but you are only minutes from your home.

Quinebaug River

Raspberries stain our mouths purple
as we gather courage to explore
the river, the Quinebaug
the only one we know.

We look for arrowheads
along the peninsula, the word
magical as we comb
the ground in our search.

We follow the brown swirling water
its musky smell to where it curves
then forks to the east and west,
white currents tumbling over rocks.

Where does it go, we ask?
Our feet planted on the grassy bank,
dreaming of far away places
we may never know.

Hickory Nuts

Be careful, mom says, zipping up our jackets
Don't talk to strangers.
Grabbing buckets, we trot downhill,
cross the bridge where whitewater churns over the dam,
the roar of the river in our ears as we walk up Mooth's Hill.

We pluck hickory nuts snug in thick brown husks,
peel some, crush inner shells with a hefty stone
for tender morsels inside,
savor the bits of tastiness.
The air smells of dusty leaves and sunshine.

When our pails are almost full, a black pick-up truck
approaches, the driver slows down watching us.
We remember what our mother said and turn our backs.
Don't talk to strangers, it might be the hunter.
The hunter, the hunter we sing.

Mudhole

To get to Cortiss' Pond
my brother and I walk from Fabyan Road
into a meadow that smells of wild geraniums,
sunburnt grass almost covers my head,
wets arms, legs, clothes.

We braid dandelions, pick buttercups
pass coiled sunning snakes.
Don't, I say when he picks up a rock,
I put the buttercups under his chin,
Do you like butter? He just laughs.

At the pond we set down our knapsacks
filled with sandwiches, juice and towels
on a cool damp bank in the shade
of the maple trees and race
into the icy spring fed water.

We play all afternoon in the shallows
where the stream feeds into the pond,
swish coarse wet sand over our bodies,

swim to wash it off again,

check for leeches before the hot walk home.

Five Mile Loop

My brother and I cycle
pass dairy farms,
grazing horses and cows. Summer air
redolent of fresh manure and wildflowers.

At Aunt Olga's, a steep downhill.

Do we walk or ride past Sophie's farm,
Sophie, the eccentric lady with sixteen dogs?
If we feel adventurous, we ride lightning fast,
feet on the handlebars,
barking dogs giving chase.

Sometimes we try to sneak by on foot
but the dogs run out snarling.
Paul carries a stick.
I hold onto his waist, quivering.

Our ride is almost over

when we hear the Falls by Fabyan Bridge,

the clanging rhythms of machines from dad's mill.

one short uphill, and then home.

Haying

At the edge of the field,
the hay-baler holds my eye,
its curved prongs blackish rust,
a museum piece in deep country.

I want to grab days of summers past,
Aunt Penna leaning forward on her tractor
that grand smile on her face
as the hay-baler drops its packets
of yellow gold.

We help her stack them
in the cool darkness of the red barn.
Strands of burnt sunshine cling to our clothes
as we jump from bale to bale
until the call for supper.

Trahana

Every August when cows milk is rich and creamy
my nana makes this Greek dish from ancient times.

She wraps her long dark braid in a scarf,
smooths white sheets on tables
in her screened in porch, waits
for the dough to sour and rise.

On the first day she punches it down.
On the second day she punches it down.
On the third day she pulls out chunks the size of fists.

Then calls the children.

They have smelled the trahana ferment
and come with rolling pins to crunch chunks
into pebbly grains and crumble them
through a wooden sieve into glass jars.

They hunger for its tart earthy taste,

but long to hear stories of shepherds

who tended their flocks in the wildflower valleys

of the Pindus Mountains, trahana in their pouches.

Their mother toasts the grains in butter,

adds paprika, water to make a gravy,

adds crusty bread,

places the pan on a shelf to cool.

Trahana Trahana. It is ready.

Country Road in the Quiet Corner

the Still River is
partially hidden

seeming to spill its banks
in a suspended motion

dragonfly wings sway
on the water's surface

insects buzz
in the green brush

looking west
the river a waterfall

silvery like midsummer rain

Crow Haven

On the way to the lake cottage
off the gravel road
on neighbors' grassy lawns
we see crows spread their inky wings
fly away three or four at a time.

Hours later, leaving the cottage,
we see them land again
walking in stately fashion,
as if they owned the place.

Memorial Day 1952

My mother in a white linen suit
holds the baby stroller. Neighbors
and children in our Sunday best

wait in front of the PO/General Store
for Veterans in Uniform and the VFW Band
to unpack drums, bugles, trumpets

for the Memorial Day march to Fabyan Cemetery.
As the sergeant reads the honor roll,
I grasp my mother's hand.

Johnny Pietluck, Theodore Angelo,
Vangel Constantine, soldiers from our village
killed on the Pacific front.

We join the parade following the Girl Scouts
with their yellow bandanas, the Boy Scouts
who hoist American flags from their belts.

At the cemetery veterans assemble

among the gravestones of the combat dead,

they too like statues.

I stop at the edge of the road. When the bugler

plays TAPS, I brace myself for the three-gun salute,

the sound of casings dropping on the grass.

The Trees

When you see the tall trees
the towering maple, the sycamore

when you hear the trees
you know you are in Fabyan Village.

I have watched these trees
whisper and tell stories.

I have seen them take over land
where houses have been abandoned.

At the corner of highway 101
and Fabyan Road

a once grand Victorian now dark gray
and skeletal is barely seen through circling trees.

Mr. Eno's elegant colonial was left to decline
new owners left it to brown and decay

shutters rotted, the roof sagged

frames of windows broken.

The trees grew larger and leafier,

thick trunked maples multiplied,

tall upright elms slowly covered the house

and the land became resplendent with dark beauty.

Little Bit of Heaven Farm

Fabyan 2017

On a sloping hill,

two brown geldings and a black mare,

their coats sleek and shining

as they move in the morning sun.

Nearer the road three Shetland ponies

two chestnuts, and one brown and white graze,

their shaggy manes touch the ground.

Lone Maple

A lone maple stands lakeside.
Two weeks ago
two sturdy maples were felled
for a better view of the lake.

I knew these trees
spent childhood summers
reading under their shade,
listening to their sounds
along with the lake's ripples.

When thunderstorms came across the lake
their vibrant green was drenched in rain.
They tossed and turned in the wind

I felt their spirit
even their protection.

I wonder if the lone maple misses the others
their breathy sounds
maybe even secrets shared.

Sitting it its shade
I feel bereft.
Does it sense my grief?

Wildflower

Deep rose veins, hollow plum pouch
cleft in the center: a solitary ladyslipper
in the pine woods.

My brother whispers, *Don't pick it.*
It only has one seed. We kneel
by the sacred altar, lightly touching petals.

At home we tell our mother about our treasure.
Wild violets grew in her homeland, she says,
by mountain streams.

In the spring we plant bluebells by the stone wall
in our backyard, watch them grow.
Tiny violet blue cups edged with deep rose.

Wildflower is my secret name.

Woodstock Orchards

Four of us visit the orchard
every September, overripe apples
battered and brown on the ground.

We inhale their musty aromas,
climb high branches
to pick bright red shiny ones,
plunk them into bushel baskets to take home,
imagining pies, dumplings, apple cider.

Mother says the peelings on the kitchen table
tell fortunes,
bring us good luck.

But they do not foretell grief.
Patty becoming a stranger. Paul's early death.

Requiem

To Paul

I spent years
exploring where the wind blows
hoping for a west wind a sweet wind

That was before the tragedy
that caught you in the winds of time
in the machine spinning wheel
dear brother
all hope gone
your light with mine

Pain is a furtive teacher
leading me from shadowlands
through moonlit dreams
that bring your spirit near

Finally –
iridescent as a child's joy
the wheel turns.

Familiar

I saw a young man
crossing White Street
as I was crossing.
He resembled
my brother Paul
who died twenty-five years ago.

I smiled and said, "Hi."
He said, "Do I know you?
You look familiar."

He had that quiet unassuming smile,
friendly, warm up to the eyes,
my brother Paul's smile.

Are you from around here?
Yes, I said.

He said he played in a band.
"Look me up.
Beelzebub.org."

Montana Reverence

We pass alpine meadows of wildflowers,
blue gentian, elephant head, paintbrush,
hike switchback trails in and out of rain.

Vast landscapes startle me into reverence,
soothes me into wholeness. Mountain goats,
white dots on jagged cliffs watch us climb.

We reach Headquarters Pass late afternoon,
dense fog drifts on the rocky ledges.
Silent prayers answered

when a headwind blows away the mist.
Sun lights far western peaks, one by one.
In the clearing two western bluebirds hover.

Stunned, I sense my brother near me
before the trails are drenched in rain
before the first step back.

Mountain Wildflower

Its white blossoms
more delicate than rainbows
grace the Alpine Garden.
Huddled in between crevices
rooted in rocks
curled leaves sheltered
by an undercoat of brown fuzz,
it grows low to escape winter storms.

You should not be deceived
by its miniature size,
it has all it needs to hunker down and survive.
I am told the leaves are used
for Labrador Tea.
How elegant to drink a cup of amber
listening to mountain winds.

Wild Music

When I walk downhill to the bridge,
I can hear the echo of machines clanging
in my mind
weaving worsteds, cashmeres, garbadines.
I hear the rush of the river.

My dad's first mill went down
into the swirling waters of the Quinebaug
in the flood of fifty five.

I still smell raw wool and grease,
see my aunts Olga and Penna sewing and spinning,
my mother finishing the cloth checking for flaws.

Now no mill waste sullies the waters;
the Quinebaug is lazy and clean.
In the broken dam trees grow in cracks,
water churns only through the trough.

On the day of Hurricane Carol
when the bridge came down

and the mill collapsed

machine parts washed down in the fierce current

with rooftops and dead pigs.

The people of Fabyan Village stood

numb on top of the hill.

I held the motion picture camera

as steady as I could

filming the devastation

until a fireman yelled, "Inside. Get inside."

Telephone wires came down

like whips in the rain.

 In the comforting shelter of home

my mother and father talked low in the dark room

planning their next move,

another mill, another place.

The mill built by my father and Uncle Louie

destroyed – their dream, our livelihood.

Now when I walk down to the Quinebaug,

it is packed with fish.

Fishermen cast their lines from the bridge,

kayakers put in beyond the dam

and in the empty space where the mill once stood

an artesian spring gushes clear water.

Lessons From My Father

When my father was teaching me how to drive
he got me so nervous
I kept stalling the car.

I drove as far as Beno's convenience store
as he yelled instructions in my ear.
Then I stopped and he took over.

But there were other times
when he took me to the window
to show me the arrival of a new bird,

when he drove me around the backroads
so I could collect money for the Red Cross,
watching to be sure I was safe from the barking dogs.

Years later I realized how hard he worked
seven days a week, long hours to keep the mill going,
getting new orders, afraid the business would fold.

He told me stories nights at the Colonial Club,

after seeing mom in the hospital. I got to know him then.

Waiting

In my yard fuzzy magnolia buds
wait for the first sun soaked day
to burst into blossom

It has been a year since the heady aroma
from the last bloom zapped my senses
on the walkway to my house

I am waiting
to tuck my face again
into petals of creamy pink
loveliness
before all too soon
they are brown slivers
on the grass

Santorini Blue

My father fit right in
jaunty fisherman's cap, weathered skin
ageless at eighty-five. My mother was from the North
but their last journey together was in the Cyclades.
Distraught for a year after her death,
he had one wish – to go back.
I took care of his hurt leg and fatigue
but the real medicine was Greece.

We taxied daily to a cafe on the caldera
enveloped by blue,
listening to Theodorakis litanies.
We gazed down at an unwrinkled sea,
light transforming us.

Hungry Fur

He doesn't like Poseidon Taverna.
There's no one here – but I persuade him.

We wait for a long time to be served
our prawns greasy and whiskered.
I eat a few with a glass of retsina
while Dad secretly tosses his from the table.

Within minutes we have visitors –
more than a dozen cats and kittens
tiny gray ones with bristled hair
skinny blacks with green eyes, sooty whites

spotted tabbies and tangerines
with tails waving high.
We are surrounded by endearing beauty.

Fira Harbor

At Fira Harbor boats come in
donkeys are laden with cargo,
look festive with braided and ribboned manes
as shepherds coax them uphill to Fira Town.

I snap pictures reach out to pet them.
My mother told us stories of her donkey's
stubbornness and devotion, their long walks,
her sadness when she left for America.

Later in the Santorini twilight
Dad and I see the herd trot by our hotel
free of burden, heading to pasture.
We hear the tinkle of bells.

Selina's

Our last night in Santorini
Dad limps down the white marble steps
to Fira's famous restaurant.

The waiter runs up, takes his hand.
"Outside?" he asks.

Yes, we nod, enchanted by the long pier
jutting into the Aegean
white linen tablecloths ruffling.

Waves lap the pier.
Strong winds blow.
It is too raw.

We race inside
to a quiet elegance of piano music,
vases of red roses on tables and mantels.

The glass door clicks us in

Call

Snow falling drifting
heavy on trails, skiing all day.
Before the candlelight dinner
the call came.

Come home now.
Your father is dying.

No passport to board a plane;
no car to drive.
Helpless until help came,

A woman I just met.
I'll drive you to the hospital.

On the five hour drive down,
we didn't talk much.

I ran in to see him. Tears rushing.
Dad

Torrential rain. Torrential love.

To Nana

We walk to Oia from Fira
on the island of Santorini
up and up white-washed stairs,
pass an old man singing
a lament at his doorstep.
Greek light all around.

Then we are lost having no map
and ask a man the way to Oia.
He points. Go down these stairs
then turn right at the grandmother.

We pass her sitting placidly
in the shade of a tree
in mourning clothes
headscarf to shoes
all black

reminding me of my grandmothers,
and the grandmothers of the world
marking the way

when we need direction
with their solidarity
devoted smiles
unconditional love.

Delphi

On Mount Parnassus I walk the Sacred Way
to the Temple of Apollo
its columns bleached to bone.

Long ago, the Pithia, high priestess
uttered the eternal message:
Gnosi Afton – Know Thyself

Processions came from Athens, Thessaloniki to hear
her prophecy and vision.
She held the Greek world in thrall.

Cypress trees, tall slim sentinels, guard the site.
I stay until the violet sunset –
watch the eagles soar and screech overhead.

Baptism, Falarsanna Bay

I make the sign of the cross
as my mother did
and her mother before her,

wade into the bay
until I am waist deep in azure, light everywhere.

I swim to where the waves crest in threes
dive through them as they turn:
triple blessings.

A baptism unlike the first one
when the priest plunged my naked body
sobbing and kicking into the tub of redemption.

Floating for hours, waves caress my body,
eons of Greek light filter through my skin.

At sunset the sky changes,
bold vertical bands of cobalt
almost touch the sea.

Gentle tides bring me to the shore.

Bells ring from the church in the hills.

It will be hard to leave this place.

Melina's Taverna

Walking from Red Beach
after swimming in the crystalline sea
we climb over rust colored cliffs
to lunch at Melina's Taverna
near the site of Akrotiri.

A child is fishing on the pier,
where the owner leads us to a wooden
table by the sea. He asks us to pick out
our own fresh bream for him to grill.

Children are playing cards in
laughing in the dark back room.
A black lab barks,
surf crackles rocks on the shore.

My mother often said,
people in the old country were not poor in spirit.
When she left Northern Epirus her family
cut strings of attachment.

One remaining string carried me back

to see what was lost. The family at the table

next to us nod and smile. We share fish and bread,

a finale of raki and something sweet.

Northern Borders

On the outskirts of Metsovo, near Albania
the tour bus pulls in for gas.
We are in north Epirus and it is my birthday.

 In the cafe I notice men with craggy faces
 in wool caps smoking, talking, laughing,
 Faces I have seen before.

Songs of Epirus play on the stereo:
the liquid strings of the oud,
the lament of the clarinet.

At the counter I drink cups of espresso,
quell the urge to get up and dance.
Later buy *Northern Borders* to take home.

On the bus our guide, Stavros, says,
"Varvara, read us your Greek poems."
I read about kourambeithes I made with my mother,

the country she left when she was twelve.

A mile away is the village of Konitza.

Across that border my mother was born.

Konitza

for my mother 1981

Wind bristles before the thunder.
The river Aoös a ribbon of green
barely seen in mist.

Your childhood friend, Fortina
asks me to lie down on the russet couch
cream lace on its arms,
a thicker lace on windows
facing the Pindus Mountains.

The thunderstorm comes. I hear it come.
I feel strangely at home when
Fortina tells me stories I've heard before:
your donkey decorated with wildflowers,
week-long wedding feasts,
a hard life with your father away for years.

A mile from here is Albania,
the white church you went to as a child.
The guard at the border remembers your father.

Fortina puts a cool cloth on my forehead,
gives me sweets: loukomi, koulourakis.
She talks of school days with you
when there was laughter and singing,
before the closing of Greek schools
before the threat of war.

Your father came back when you were twelve,
and you left this alpine valley,
your uncles and grandmother forever.

Picnics with your donkey
the white church
the gray stone farmhouse:
I have this to take with me.

Tsiftiteli

In the ornate cedar chest
a red embroidered bedspread
pillow cases of silk and lace
pink quartz tumblers for sweet wine

I lift my arms to dance the tsiftiteli
touching ancient cities
countryside of olive hills turquoise seas
Greece breathed in breathed out.

A flower ring of white anemones
on my hand, I awaken
to the music of the lyra and laouto.
I don't need a dowry.

The Closing of G. Thomas and Sons

David should have closed the mill years before he did.
He kept trying to keep it going even as the industry waned.
He didn't want to let the family name down.

He kept trying to keep it going even after Paul's tragedy
in the mill – that moment of terror
when he got caught in the spinner.

He had come from California
He lived in a trailer in Santa Rosa,
 brought a girlfriend with him to Connecticut.

He ran the mill for twenty-six years
dealing with a broken heart,
drinking – artist in disguise.

He wove blankets, tablecloths, high end fabrics,
hustling for work, losing money
till he had to shut the mill down.

He finally sold it to a good man with a good idea.

G. Thomas and Sons became Thomas Commons:

a children's dance studio, a hair salon, a cafe.

David began a new life, and painted thirty five swirling pieces

 in half a year, a few hanging in the cafe.

We go there sometimes for coffee and a sandwich,

sitting on the patio in the spring, by the fireplace in winter.

Changes

Fishermen use the cleaned up Quinebaug
to catch trout; kayakers launch from a new landing

near the sturdy bridge
built after the flood of '55 after dad's mill went down.

Looms and machine parts washed downriver.
along with dead animals, rooftops, debris.

The Post Office/General Store closed years ago;
no more waiting by the bronze veterans' plaque

to march with the parade on Memorial Day
the quarter mile to the cemetery.

Across the street two small houses have replaced
Mr. Eno's once elegant white colonial.

My brother David lives in our sturdy home
retired, carrying on with painting and metal sculpture.

Mr. Prince sold his ten-acre farm at the junction
of Fabyan Road and Highway 131,

 the Little Bit of Heaven Farm,
a new blessing where I stop to watch

the horses and the Shetland ponies
graze unaware of their own beauty.

Little seems changed but much has
on this road winding through the valley.

The Quiet Corner the only darkness in the sky
on an Atlantic coast sparkling with industrial light.

Along Fabyan Road
the night sky is filled with stars.

Kombaloi

The worry beads in my hand
fall one onto the other
click click in a slow rhythm.

They subdue heartache
promise smooth passages
in the everydayness of life.

Some are souvenir white and blue
but mine are antique amber,
delicate to touch.

I bought them in a little shop in Oia
overlooking the sea, while dad
waited impatiently for me.

He didn't know stories of kombaloi
tell the history of Greece,
its music, its anguish.

My grandfather flips and tosses

square chunky orange beads
on the armchair by the window,

maybe thinking of the country he left.
I finger and toss the silk russet tassel
caressing the country I found.

About the Author

Barbara Thomas grew up in The Last Green Valley. She earned a Masters Degree From Boston University in Education and taught English and Reading in the public schools for 35 years. While a special student at Harvard University, School of Education she wrote an award winning program, *Literature, Life-Cycle and Inner-Stories* for high school students. She is active in the Boston/Cambridge poetry community and has given many poetry readings and workshops, and nature-writing walks. While studying at the Joiner Institute's Writers Conference, she was invited to participate in the Jeff Male Memorial Reading for publishing the chapbook, *Seduced by Sighs of Trees,* Cloudkeeper Press, 2007. She has also published work in *The Paterson Literary Review,* 2015-2016, *Fiele-Festa,* (online 2015), *Lalitamba,* 2006, the *Greek-Institute Newsletter, Writing Nature, Small Press Review, Bagel Bard Anthology #4,* and other journals.

"Rich in evocative detail, Barbara Thomas's new book juxtaposes geographies and generations, one green valley nesting inside another. The poet opens the book and later returns it to her mother's birthplace in a borderland that once was Greece; in between, she revisits her own childhood in a nearly Edenic Connecticut lush landscape, fondly depicted relatives, and tempting foods are the stuff of Thomas's memories. But an inescapable awareness that both places and people are gone gradually makes loss the inseparable but profound companion of memory."

—Martha Collins

"This book of poems is a celebrations of wholeness and completion. Beginning with parent and grandparents emigrating from northern Greece, and ending with the poet herself glimpsing the valley they came from, Barbara Thomas draws a wide circle of affirmation. Within it is 'air so fresh you can taste it' and wildflowers 'more delicate than rainbows.' Within that circle are stories of struggle and endurance, loss and death. There are also signs and hints that suggest we are sustained by the love and abiding care we have witnessed in those who have come before. *The Last Green Valley* puts us in touch with that essential and humane wellspring of heart."

—Fred Marchant

"In Barbara Thomas's very beautiful poem, '*Northern Epirus*,' her mother offers a passing remembrance of the dispossessed place of her origin, her village by the Aoös River, as 'Air so fresh you can taste it.' Everywhere in this dignified book one can taste the freshness of cadences as utterly unforced and as delicately modulated as the breath of loss itself made vivid transcription. The flow of lucid language, like the flow of the Aos River that leads directly into her own American childhood of growing up by the Quinebaug River, and of her father's doomed mill, and all the minutely recorded particulars of one landscape recalling the particulars of the other long gone overseas one. And then there's that other river the River of Oblivion, kept at bay, at least by the Orphic registers of poetry. The delicate power in the poetry of Barbara Thomas recalling, through the recipes of ancient Greek traditions, the way to preserve the family gathering."

—George Kalogeris